TALES OF THE LITE

A RIDGE TOO FAR AND OTHER STORIES

VIVEK ANANTHAKRISHNAN

First Published in April 2023

ISBN: 978-93-5741-577-4

BLUEROSE PUBLISHERS

www.BlueRoseONE.com

info@bluerosepublishers.com

+91 8882 898 898

Cover Design:

Muskan Sachdeva

Typographic Design:

Rohit

Distributed by: BlueRose, Amazon, Flipkart

Dedication

To all the Officers and men of the Sikh Light Infantry and the Indian Army, I had the privilege of serving with. And to my family!

DISCLAIMER

Tales of the Lite: A Ridge Too Far and other stories is a work of fiction. All incidents and dialogue, and all characters with the exception of some well-known historical figures and incidents, are products of the author's imagination and are not to be construed as real. Where real-life historical figures appear, the situations, incidents, and dialogues concerning those persons are entirely fictional and are not intended to depict actual events or to change the entirely fictional nature of the work. In all other respects, any resemblance to actual persons, living or dead, events, or locales is entirely coincidental.

The opinions expressed are those of the characters and should not be confused with the author.

The book is purely fiction and we do not intend to hurt the sentiments of any individual, community, sect, or religion.

No part of this publication may be reproduced, distributed, or transmitted in any form or by any means, including photocopying, recording, or other electronic or mechanical methods, without prior permission of the author.

FOREWORD

I have known Colonel Vivek Ananthakrishnan, Sena Medal, since the time we were subalterns together in the 7th Battalion, The Sikh Light Infantry. Having shared many experiences together, I can say with certainty that he has many splendid qualities including an eye for detail, a sense of humour and above all, the ability to empathise with others.

All these facets are amply illustrated in this collection of short stories. They bring to the fore the human element in all of us. When people look at us, they see only the man in the uniform, stern and steely. Very few see the man behind the uniform, who has his own unique emotions and relationships. An obedient son, a doting father, a carefree youth, the possibilities are endless. Each story delves into the deeper aspects of human nature and shows how in our heart of hearts, we are all human, bound together with a strong sense of camaraderie.

I wish Colonel Vivek Ananthakrishnan all the very best and look forward to many more such offerings.

Happy Reading.

New Delhi   General Manoj Naravane,
                   (Retd)

Mar 2023   PVSM, AVSM, SM, VSM, ADC

FOREWARD

I am extremely privileged to introduce the book A RIDGE TOO FAR AND OTHER STORIES written by the very talented writer Col Vivek Ananthakrishnan, Sena Medal.

Throughout the pages of this book, you find a collection of stories that are true and deeply inspiring but also entertaining. Each story is a testament to the power of human spirit, the resilience of, human heart and the strength of human will.

As I read through each story, I found myself becoming more and more engaged, caught up with the characters journey and their struggles. I was moved by their triumphs and inspired by their courage in the face of adversity.

The author's ability to convey complex emotions and ideas through these stories is truly remarkable. The storytelling is elegant as it is masterful and often, I was reflecting on the epilogues at the end of each story. The poignant account of army life and its tribulations have been presented showing profound humanism.

It's truly a collection of stories that will resonate with you and will leave you feeling uplifted. It is hope built on one fact -SURVIVAL as the author puts it.

I invite you to enjoy the incredible stories written by Col Vivek and I am sure you will not be disappointed.

Bangalore Regards,

Mar 2023   Dr Manjula Raman

ACKNOWLEDGEMENTS

I want to express my gratitude towards the amazing people who have supported and encouraged me.

To my family for continuously encouraging me to write stories.

To General MM Naravane, PVSM, AVSM, SM, VSM, ADC for taking the time to write a forward for my first book.

To Dr Manjula Raman, Evangelist, Chief Knowledge Officer and Pedagogist, for taking the time to write a forward for my first book.

To Harshitha Jayavel, for patiently reading the stories and giving invaluable suggestions.

To Lt General Ashok Kapur for giving an idea that led to the short story "The Valley Across the River".

To the veterans, especially Colonel Harjit Singh, the master historian, for the input on the story that led to "The Ridge too Far".

The Editorial Board of the Coach Magazine Bangalore Chapter for granting permission to republish my short story 'The Commitment."

To Varun Krishnan and Deepika Rawat of Blue Rose publishers for the dedicated effort and assistance in publishing the book.

To Muskaan Sachdeva for the excellent cover design.

And to Lt Col Ramesh Menon for encouraging me all the way.

PREFACE

"Never a dull moment."

The above quote of an old timer from my Regiment typifies the life we spent.

Most stories in this book have their roots there. Stories that started from small ideas and anecdotes.

As I spent time with corporate clients as a Master Trainer Facilitator and later as a Coach (ICF), I realized that many of these stories had immense lessons about human fortitude, resilience, interpersonal relations, and emotions.

CONTENTS

GLOSSARY

Artillery-Denotes large-calibre guns used in warfare on land.

Battery -An artillery subunit of guns, men, and vehicles.

Barakhana- A periodic get-together of the officers and troops.

BFNA -Battlefield Nursing Assistants. Soldiers trained as Nursing staff to give first aid to casualties.

Bunker-A bunker is a shelter, usually, underground, that has strong walls to protect the people inside it from bullets or bombs. Generally made with stones and material readily available.

Commandos are a small group of soldiers specially trained to make attacks on enemy areas that are dangerous or difficult to attack.

Defended post- the position held by a small element, e.g., an infantry section. Posts are grouped in mutual support to form defended localities.

Field Engineers also called sappers. Sappers are trained in various tasks, including bridge-building, clearing explosive hazards, creating obstacles, demolitions, and operating small boats.

First light -The time when light first appears in the morning, dawn.

Hotel hour- H hour- The time of day an attack, landing, or any military operation is scheduled to begin.

Howitzers -A short gun for firing shells on high trajectories at low velocities. These are commonly used in the mountains.

Indian Army Commissioned Officer Ranks- Field Marshal, General, Lieutenant General, Major General, Brigadier, Colonel, Lieutenant Colonel, Major, Captain, Lieutenant.

Indian Army Junior Commissioned Officers (JCOs) - Are entrusted with supervisory roles, and the three JCO ranks are Subedar Major, Subedar, and Naib Subedar.

Indian Army Non-Commissioned Officers (NCOs) are enlisted soldiers with specific skills and duties such as training, recruiting, and military policing, and the three NCO ranks are Havildar, Naik, and Lance naik.

Indian Army Unit/sub-units:

Section -Commanded by Havildar, involving ten men.

Platoon- Commanded by Captain/Lieutenant / Junior Commissioned Officer (JCO), including (Three) 3 Sections.

Company (Rifle) -Commanded by Major, comprising Three (3) Platoons.

Battalion -Commanded by Colonel/Lt Colonel, consisting of around 900 men divided into Four (4) Rifle Companies.

Brigade -Commanded by Brigadier, comprising Three (3) Battalions and Support Elements

Division -Commanded by Major General, comprising Three to four (3-4) Brigades.

Last light -Astronomical dusk, the time after sunset when the sky becomes completely dark.

Line of Control (LC) -A line that is supposed to indicate the boundary between the part of the Indian state of Kashmir and the Pakistan occupied areas of Kashmir.

Machine guns. An automatic weapon that fires bullets in rapid succession for as long as the trigger is pressed. The reference is to light and medium machine guns.

Mines- a weight-triggered explosive device intended to maim or kill people or to disable or destroy vehicles.

Minefield - an area of land or water that contains mines

Pioneers - The Pioneer regiments in the British Army were specialised infantry rather than engineers. Regarded as among the elite, they were additionally skilled in road and railway building and their abilities. (Refer to Indian Army Pioneer Regiments of the British Army)

PRC or AN/PRC 77 Radio Set is a manpack, portable VHF FM combat-net radio transceiver used to provide short-range, two- way radio telephone voice communication.

Quarter Master- An army officer/JCO/NCO who provides clothing and subsistence for a body of troops.

Shelling- the heavy artillery fire to saturate an area rather than hit a specific target.

Stand to -A state of readiness assumed by ground troops at dawn and dusk in wartime.

WD - Cable used for landlines by the Army.

A RIDGE TOO FAR

Prologue

The men of Alpha Company lay hidden behind boulders along a narrow spur, having crawled up in the snow once the darkness set in. The men waited and watched the enemy. There was no wind that night, yet the cold was numbing. The line of enemy stone bunkers was visible, silhouetted in a clear sky. All seemed quiet and peaceful.

To their West, a few hundred yards away, along a steep spur line, hidden among the thick bushes and cherry trees, lay a small group of men. They were the Commandos, the toughest of the battalion. Separating them from the line of enemy bunkers was a minefield.

The men waited for the Hotel hour.

A Quiet Place

The battalion had moved into this region the previous year. The men were from the border areas of the state of

Punjab. They owed their lineage to the Pioneers who fought in Abyssinia, Afghanistan, China and both the World Wars. Tough and hardened soldiers with minimal wants. They were the true sons of the soil.

The Line of Control (LC) over here protruded into the enemy area like a hump. A centuries-old trade route connecting the Valley cut across the lesser Himalayas through a famous mountain pass in the Southwest. This mountain pass had been captured in the previous war after a hard-fought battle. When the war was over, it was given back to the enemy. The old trade route was developed as a National Highway and passed through a small township, the Southwestern Gateway to the Valley that lay astride the Jhelum.

Two ridgelines emanated from the same peak in the enemy area. One ran in an East-to-West direction where the battalion had taken up defences. This ridgeline with heights ranging between eight to ten thousand feet ASL tapered down towards the banks of the Jhelum overlooking the township. The LC ran parallel to this ridgeline to its South. From the enemy-occupied area, the other ridgeline intersected the LC in a Southeast direction.

The men were not unduly worried about the enemy. The towering ridgeline with a helmet-shaped peak in the enemy area, looming high over the LC, held their attention. The entire ridgeline dwarfed the defended areas on their side of the LC. The Helmet Top was over 11000 feet and seemed unoccupied by the enemy. Higher up to the Southeast, on the same ridgeline, were the defended posts of the enemy. Along these posts ran an alternate road that connected to the main route.

The days passed, and the artillery shelling and sporadic spurts of firing along the LC by the enemy indicated it all. The war in the East was now almost ten months old. War breaking out in the West was just a matter of time. History was about to witness the birth of a new nation.

The battalion started recalling all the soldiers on leave as it was time to regroup and prepare for the inevitable war.

A time when plans were made, directed, and choreographed in the divisional headquarters. Strict control reigned on battalion moves except for routine activities.

The plan seemed quite simple. Occupy the Helmet-Top, if unoccupied by the enemy. Capture, if occupied.

The plan hinged on the initial intelligence reports that suggested the opposition would be nonexistent or minimal. The assessment in the Divisional Operations room about the enemy defences and battle plan also concurred with the intelligence reports of the likelihood of the Helmet top not being occupied.

As part of the divisional battle plans, Warning Orders were also issued for the capture of the Helmet Top. A company with the commando platoon was tasked to attack and capture the Helmet-Top.

The Alpha Company holding defences in depth were relieved for this task. The Charlie Company on the LC was designated as a reserve. The attack was going to be assisted by fire support from a battery of mountain howitzers and a platoon of field engineers.

The company set about their task in earnest, sometimes in full view of the enemy.

Waiting for the Storm

The days meandered at a languid pace.

In such trying times, soldiers do find ways to relieve stress.

The company officer of Delta Company, a bit of a Bollywood actor in his previous avatar, kept the officers in splits through a longer part of the night.

So too, the soldiers. Wondered how many would live to see daylight again.

Meanwhile, the Alpha Company and the commando platoon prepared for battle.

The dapper young Major commanding Alpha Company had forged a formidable outfit and knew the men well. A master of many operations in the Eastern sector, he knew that surprise would be difficult to maintain. Success would depend on a lot of other factors.

It was also unlikely that his troops sitting below could observe any reinforcements and other activities of the enemy.

The Alpha company moved into its final location and prepared to launch into operations.

After a few days, the orders for the attack were put on hold.

A month passed. It was almost December. The commando platoon continued its plan to probe the enemy defences wherever possible. Soon they had a taste of action when they came under intense enemy fire a few times for venturing too close.

In early December, around dinner time, the night sky lit up with the tracer rounds of machine guns being fired incessantly into the bunkers. The enemy artillery also commenced shelling the bunkers on the LC.

War was now officially announced in the West. The long wait seemed over. Alpha company and the commando platoon made final preparations and moved close to the LC.

The battalion now awaited final orders. Everything hinged on the thought process of the Higher Headquarters and their reading of the battle.

None but the Brave

The commandos had moved as close to the LC as possible towards the East, unseen by the enemy.

They were to carry out an outflanking move from the East, infiltrate through a minefield and take the enemy by surprise.

The commando platoon commander was a handsome and powerfully built young Captain. He had grown up in a large teak tree estate in the Western Ghats owned by his father. His father had settled there after the partition. He had sinews of steel in his forearms, fashioned by chopping logs as a pastime in his younger days. He was also polyglot and comfortable in various local languages.

Meanwhile, fresh orders from the higher headquarters arrived. The commando platoon was ordered to capture the helmet top that night.

They crossed the LC and commenced their ascent. Smaller groups could move faster over the roughest terrain. The soldiers familiar with the lie of the land rapidly moved close to their objective.

Soon they would encounter the minefield laid close to the enemy defences.

However, another obstacle in the shape of the higher HQ reared its head. A fresh set of orders had been issued. The commando platoon was to observe and report. The attack would go in the following night as was planned earlier. Other attacks along the LC had also been planned simultaneously.

The commandos settled in to observe like a patrol. Patrols are routinely tasked to gauge the extent of enemy defences, the approximate number of enemy soldiers, machine guns and minefields and so on.

The commando platoon observed some enemy activity. They waited and watched and collected the necessary information.

If they moved now, they could get across the LC before the break of the day. These few hours of darkness would give them adequate cover.

Then disaster struck. The points man moving back to lead the platoon slipped and stepped on a landmine, blowing off his leg. The platoon havildar ran to pick up the injured soldier, and as he dragged him to safety, he too stepped on a landmine.

Two explosions and the enemy now were fully alert. The machine guns opened.

The young commando platoon commander dragged his men to safety. Suddenly he felt a sharp pain in his calf, lost balance and tumbled over. He must have slipped about 100 feet down one of the spines when he realized what had happened. He had been shot. He had fallen into the minefield. He shouted to his men to take cover as he set about extricating himself from the minefield. For him, the battle was not over yet.

He was lucky that the bullet had gone through his calf. Using his strong arms, he slowly pulled himself up the slope. The going was slow as he could not risk dislodging any stray mine. After about an hour, he was back with his men. Slowly the men pulled back into their defences.

Far Far the Mountain Peak

The Alpha company had moved close to the LC at night. The battle for the helmet top ridge was now to go in at night.

The company was all set to attack past midnight. The latest assessment of the enemy was about 25 to 30 in strength spread along the helmet top. The plans had been made and rehearsed. Yet battle has so many imponderables, and nothing could be expected to go as planned.

With so much going on in the past few days, the element of surprise looked bleak. Attacking a steep gradient was going to be another challenge. The odds were stacking up slowly.

In this deadly place, it was here that the Alpha company and the commando platoon were to charge in.

At the Hotel hour, the howitzers in fire support for the assault commenced bombarding the Helmet-Top. Alpha company, led by their Company Commander, began their assault from the North. The commando platoon, led by their platoon commander, who had patched up his wound by then, was back in the thick of the action. The original plan was to simultaneously attack the South, East, and Central portions of the Helmet Top.

This time the enemy was waiting. The enemy opened with all their machine guns, severely impeding the progress. The Company Commander had to now decide on his next move. He decided to tackle the helmet top piecemeal in three phases.

The plan was that the fire support of the howitzers was to lift after 15 minutes, by which time the Alpha company would have reached the Helmet top. With a change in plan, ideally, fire support was required to pound the Southern and Eastern portions of the Helmet top. This would prevent the enemy from disrupting the attack.

The Company Commander was in for another setback. His PRC radio set had taken a burst of medium machine gun fire. Communication with the Artillery was out of the question.

The Company Commander decided to continue without artillery fire support. There was no time to lose, for he had already reached so far.

Whatever said, it was a brave decision considering all the odds. Later, one could appreciate how courageous the decision was, as the enemy had strengthened the defences by getting in more troops through the cover of darkness.

The night continued, and the Helmet Top witnessed heavy fighting. As men around him were cut down, the Company Commander, the remaining men and the commando platoon drove the enemy out of the Northern and Central parts of the Helmet top. What remained was the depth platoon situated in the South.

Charge of the Lites

The depth portion was located to the Southeast and was higher than the surrounding areas. It was also linked to the enemy's main defences, from where the enemy could quickly get reinforcements.

Sunrise was just a few hours away.

The attack stalled. The Company Commander could now either hold positions or wait for reinforcements.

Charlie Company would have to move from the LC along the ridge line in the daylight. The move would take at least a few hours.

To resolve this stalemate, the Alpha Company Commander forced the issue. It was now or never.

Leaving half his men to hold defences, he tackled the Southern portion with about ten men.

The men of Alpha Company charged. The men were cut down as the enemy fired volley after volley. The gallant Company Commander went down with his men.

A shaken enemy realized the grim situation they were in. The enemy carried out a series of counterattacks. Slowly, the men of Alpha Company were pushed out from the North and Central portion of the Helmet Top.

The Divisional Headquarters called off the attack.

Twenty men were killed along with the Company Commander that fateful night. Many were seriously wounded.

The Commando platoon commander and what was left of his platoon spent most of the next day retrieving the bodies of his slain comrades.

A few days later, the war ended on the Western front.

Epilogue

There are those battles that are eulogized for several reasons.

For every such battle, there have been many more brutal battles.

Many get reduced to footnotes or a brief mention of history.

Many soldiers who fought such battles are forgotten.

Few would come back alive!

They also fought a battle against all odds.

So close, yet so far.

They also were among the bravest of the brave.

LOCKED DOWN

The BlackRock

The Blackrock was huge. At least 70 ft wide and 15 ft high. It hung over a ledge. It was clearly visible from the river. The portion under the rock resembled a cave. It protected the men from the enemy snipers, heavy automatics, and artillery shelling. It shielded them from rain, snow, and cold winds during inclement weather. It was here that the men had regrouped before the attack.

From the BlackRock, narrow finger-like spurs extended onto the massive ridgeline that loomed over these craggy crests. To the uninitiated, if one imagined a palm facing down on a table, the ridge line was like the knuckles and the fingers the spurs. The enemy sat on the ridgeline while we occupied the posts on the knuckles, each separated by at least a few hundred yards.

The Clouds' End

The ridge line was over 15000 ft above sea level. To the North lay the famous town the "Gateway to the Eight Thousanders".

This area was just a few miles East of the narrow pass named after the goddess of Tibetan's four seasons. This pass connected the Valley to the Cold Desert plateau and the Glacier. The severe cold and inaccessibility had ensured peace for a long time. The threat of enemy incursions was unexpected, and this entire stretch of ridgeline along the Line of Control was only patrolled seasonally.

The Glacier turned into a battlefield around the period when the Prime Minister was assassinated. The focus was now on the intermittent battle that raged on the Glacier. The enemy managed to sneak in and occupy this imposing ridgeline in this area over weeks. The incursion was only discovered when the enemy artillery shelling targeted the long convoys on the national highway.

The battle that followed was bloody and swift. Many died, yet the enemy seemed well entrenched along portions of the ridgeline. The enemy had occupied the crucial heights, and they could fire at will on the isolated posts on our defences.

The Guardian Angel

The fierce battle fought a few years before to push back the intruding enemy happened over several days. The battle was fought over different ridgelines and took a heavy toll on lives.

The platoon commander in charge of the assault to the North of the Blackrock was an ageing Junior Commissioned Officer. He was on his last tour of duty before. He was to retire to his village at the end of the month. The brave Subedar led his men with such ferocity that the enemy was pushed back to the ridgeline. Severely wounded, he returned to the Blackrock, where he died.

The legend claimed that the Blackrock was protected by his spirit. At one corner of this shelter was a stone idol with a lamp lit every evening in memory of the platoon commander. It was customary for the troops moving on to the higher posts to stop and pay obeisance before moving on.

The Mean Streets

The battalion headquarters, located close to the National Highway along a tributary of the Indus, was around 9000 ft ASL. Even in the peak of summer, the water in the river would be ice cold. By December, the river would have frozen.

The posts were all more than half a day's journey by foot. There was only one fair weather track on the other side of the river that followed the river line to the Northwest and stopped a few thousand feet below the Blackrock. The track was connected to the headquarters by a footbridge.

The climb commenced from this location. The journey to the Blackrock from this point was a steep climb. In some places, the ascent was about 80 degrees, and a rope was necessary to haul oneself up. The route along the river was scenic, and the walk to the Blackrock could be done during daylight hours too.

The move from the Blackrock to the posts along the spurs could only be made after the last light. Each post was on a different route, taking 3 to 4 hours.

Once inside the post, one had to get ready before dawn and settle down in a stone bunker till dusk. This was to be the humble abode of the Company Commander. The men were staying in a few similar stone bunkers strung along the extremities of the post. All moves in the open would attract enemy snipers' potshots and bursts of medium machine guns. Walls of hastily piled stones gave cover for a movement within the post.

A Day in the Life

Getting to the defended posts was relatively easy. After that, it was a battle between man, the elements, and the enemy. The computer revolution was yet to take off in the country. Mobiles were a distant future.

Spending time was not a challenge -it was a nightmare. All routine activities within the close confines of the post were carried out at a leisurely pace. Movement outside the defences would have challenged the Flash himself.

The company had a small ubiquitous, hardy telephone exchange that could communicate to the various posts by landline and the Battalion Headquarters. The landline would be disconnected the minute the weather got bad. Lightning had claimed enough casualties of those who were not fast enough to disengage their field telephones during thunder and lightning. Heavy rains and snowfall would disrupt the landline called the WD cable. The field telephones and exchanges, and cables were of vintage stock. The talk was restricted to routine reporting in the morning and evening or any other incident on occurrence.

The only faithful companions had been a few books and the Philips radio set used to tune in songs and news from around the world. An oil lamp could be lit inside the bunker after dark to let one eat dinner and listen to the radio.

The official letters would be delivered once a week with fresh supplies. This was when one wrote letters to friends and relatives not seen or visited for years.

Slowly one got used to living as a nocturnal animal. One would eagerly wait for dusk to visit the other posts provided weather permitted it.

Winter was around the corner. The time was to stock up on the posts and prepare for the extreme cold. Time for stocking was calculated as per the moon's rise. Dark nights were ideal for stocking up. The stocking was done by hauling the stores and food by porters and mountain ponies. Night after night, the work would continue.

The men spent the nights repairing their bunkers' tracks and protective walls.

The men had rigged up a water supply system that pumped fresh potable water from the stream to the highest post. Water would be pumped up once a day. From there on, the water pipes were used to carry water to the posts lower down. To prevent the water from freezing and pipes from bursting in winter, the pipes were insulated by jackets and buried in the ground wherever possible.

Only the Lonely

This was a lockdown in the real sense. A group of men spent time confined to small, defended posts battling against the harsh and adverse environment and a treacherous foe. The only communications with the outside world were through letters.

Hope was that one knew that the battalion's tenure would end at some point. Hope was that one could go home once in three months.

Most importantly, hope was built on one factor – Survival.

THE COMMITMENT

Prologue

This happened a long time ago. Life seemed so simple and less complicated then.

The days when the post and telegraph department was the mainstay of communication. Letters posted in villages would take a few days to be delivered. And you could be sure that it would be delivered.

Telephones were a luxury limited to the privileged.

As coaches, leaders, and specialists, I leave you to draw your lessons and conclusions from this story.

Trials and Tribulations

We had just settled into peacetime mode in a small city in Central India. Time is spent training, playing games and more training as all infantry battalions do. Summertime was on us, with longer days and shorter nights.

Walking to my company office that morning, I saw a stocky person standing outside. As I went nearer, I realized it was Amrik, my go-to man.

Amrik looked different in uniform and perfectly tied turban … or was it because I had only seen him in his boxing rig in the last few months.

Thoughts raced through my mind.

Shouldn't he be preparing for the event that evening?

Soldiers must be in full uniform for the Company Commander's formal interview. So, what was he doing dressed in uniform? Was he in trouble again?

Entering my office, I could see a perplexed-looking 2-i-C (the second in command) holding an inland letter. The 2-i-C whispered, "Sir, Amrik's father died a few days ago in his village. We just received this letter."

An occupational hazard for soldiers. I could comprehend Amrik's situation.

I remember I could not talk to my father before he died. A lot unsaid and not done.

The 2-i-C continued, "Sir, please don't tell Amrik. I implore you. We won't have an answer for the Commanding Officer."

"Why?"

"What, Sir? You know that his final bout is in the evening. He won't be in a condition to fight."

The Decision

The Brigade boxing finals were later that evening. Amrik was Alpha Company's star performer, the only representative from my Company. A gold prospect for our battalion.

Amrik was pitted against a Services welterweight runner-up, a man with a reputation for being a fierce opponent, the rival battalion's star performer.

Now, the odds seemed near impossible.

"Leave it to me," I told my 2-i-c as he looked at me in disbelief. I asked the company clerk to prepare a certificate for leave.

I called Amrik into my office and gave him the inland letter. He read it silently.

Soldiers do not make show of emotions. There were no tears. That would come later with the memories. He was the eldest son.

The burden of responsibilities was traditionally the privilege of the firstborn. So much to do, and yet not enough.

After consoling him, I said, "Here is your leave letter. I have sanctioned full leave. Rest, the choice is entirely yours. Whatever you decide, I stand by you."

These are simple folk from the border villages of Punjab, large-hearted, living their dreams as soldiers. Proud as the land they come from.

I still remember what he said that day. He said, "Sir, my father is gone. Nothing can be done now. I shall fight".

Meanwhile, I met the Commanding Officer and informed him of my actions. For once, he seemed to agree with me. I went back to routine work for the day.

The Final Bout

The tournament was being held in the open. The sweltering heat meant that the finals would commence just after sundown.

I saw the ring lit up in the distance as I hurried to the venue.

The fanfare was announcing the VIP's entrance. I just made it in time.

Amrik's bout was the first match of the evening.

Moments later, the gong sounded. Round one was on.

I spotted a vacant chair and eased myself in.

I did not get a chance to sit. It was all over before it had started.

A section of the crowd went berserk, and there I was, jumping and cheering.

It was the shortest bout I would ever witness. A KO (knockout).

Seconds into the round, Amrik unleashed a vicious short hook.

His much-fancied opponent never knew what hit him.

Amrik Singh threw his gloves away, walked up to me and said, "Sir, Can I go now?"

I nodded and just beamed.

Unwavering commitment in the faith and trust reposed is a soldier's creed.

Do what you must against all odds, for the pain is secondary,

I come last,

What matters is my commitment to the goal!!

THE LONG DARK TUNNEL

Prologue

It was a new day. The ridgelines of the Himalayas, all draped in white, are clearly visible on the horizon. The sun seemed to be shining brighter after three days of continuous snowfall.

The environment evoked calmness and serenity- a time to take stock and regroup.

And soldiers' rue –nothing is what that seems.

Ominous Signs

The second coldest inhabited place on earth lay a few miles to the East, where temperatures would plummet below minus 30 degrees centigrade. At higher altitudes, it got worse with the blizzards.

The battalion was spread 25 to 30 miles over two ridgelines perilously close to a longstanding enemy. The ridges were separated by a river and connected by a footbridge.

Access from the battalion headquarters (HQ) to the National Highway (NH) was a fair-weather dirt track.

Surviving the elements and a recalcitrant, unforgiving foe was only a part of an ongoing battle. Movement along the narrow mountain tracks was restricted to moonless nights and on reverse slopes, unseen by prying eyes and trigger-happy snipers. Yet, swift motion in ones and twos in short spurts was worth a well-taken risk.

The sound that seemed like a whiplash echoed across the valleys and mountains.

The first avalanche of the season seemed too close for comfort. A portion of the road connecting the access to the Battalion Headquarters (HQ) was now blocked.

Road clearance could take the more significant part of the day.

The Call

This Charlie Company beefed up to more than 150 men was defending the Western ridgeline. The company commander, a young Major, a veteran of many operations, had celebrated his 30th birthday the previous summer. He was well entrenched in the Saddle, his company HQs, knowing this would be a long haul for him. His concern was the section-defended post stretched out furthest from his HQ at a lower altitude, the position that took the brunt of the enemy's relentless fire assaults. Most of his time was spent organizing and rallying his men for the next battle.

The call came in around noon from Point Double Nine. The telephone lines had just been repaired. Point Double 9, or Pt 99, was the battalion's highest occupied section defended post, more than 18 thousand ft above sea level.

Balli Singh, the bard, the Quarter Master, had been taken ill in the morning. The details still needed to come in.

Everyone knew him, yet most of the soldiers couldn't remember his real name. Some said it was the village Balli where he was born; others noted that it was an abbreviated version of Balwinder,

Yet, he was the only "Balli" known for his bawdy songs after each meeting with the Pirate and the Monk at the monthly battalion barakhanas (get-togethers).

The medic available was an infantry soldier, trained as a Battlefield Nursing Assistant (BFNA), in other words, a nurse capable of first aid and faithfully reporting symptoms to the Doc. The BFNA was the next best bet when the Doc was not available. The Doc was on the other ridgeline. In the best weather, reaching the river line would take him at least eight hours of non-stop walking.

The company officer, a young Lieutenant fresh from the Academy, and the medic were already moving up from the Company Headquarters. It would take a few hours for them to reach Point Double 99.

The SOPs were getting activated. Executive orders were being issued. Evacuation in case required.

The Verdict

The report from the BFNA came in. He had a series of conversations with the Doc. Shortly after, the Doc gave his verdict. It seemed, in all probability, a case of the dreaded HACO- High Altitude Cerebral Edema. The Balli would have to be evacuated.

For the soldier, any delay meant certain death.

Evacuations evoked a sense of dread in the Company Commander.

An incident occurred when the Major was leading a reconnaissance patrol in the north of an island country. The points man of the patrol stepped on a stone and tripped over a mine, severing his femoral vein. The points-man, yet to cross his teens, bled out on the Major's lap, waiting for a helicopter evacuation that came too late. That was another time and place, another country, someone else's war! Those memories would continue to haunt him time and again.

Another battle was in progress a few hundred kilometres to the East -in the glacier.

Most of the helicopters were on sorties ferrying stores and casualty evacuation.

The earliest a helicopter could only arrive was first light the following day.

Helicopter night flying capabilities for higher altitudes were not a reality yet.

The helipad was at the confluence of the river at an altitude of about 8000 feet. The journey by foot from Double 9 would take approximately seven hours of non-stop walking. This also involved negotiating a particularly nasty piece of terrain named Rockfall on the route from the Saddle Headquarters to the helipad.

Carved into a cliff face, the Rockfall was a hundred-metre narrow track with just enough space for one man to walk. The other side was a sheer drop of a few thousand feet.

An alternate roundabout route used by the mules to ferry the stores also existed. Evacuation would have to be done by that route. That would take about 10 to 11 hours.

Home Run

The stage was set. The entire battalion was on "stand-to". Men were ready to move. The move required stealth and speed. A race to beat inclement weather, use the darkness, avoid a watchful and trigger-happy enemy, and save the life of a brother.

The Doc was also ready to move down towards the helipad.

The Balli had to be saved.

The Company Commander was waiting for the last light. That time after sunset and before total darkness. The earliest they could start.

The moon was in the third quarter. Moonrise would be around midnight –five hours of darkness to move the men.

As darkness crept in, the men sprang into action. It was a race like never, ever before.

The Lieutenant came racing down the narrow mountain track with his party carrying the casualty. The next group took over at the Saddle. This process was to continue time and again over the route. Fresh pair of legs waited at each checkpoint. There was no rest, and the night seemed longer than ever.

Crisis brings out the best in teamwork. No questions were asked as each man did more than his bit. Suddenly everything seemed like a well-choreographed sequence.

At the break of day, as the evacuation party turned around the bend in the track and saw the footbridge, Doc's party was racing in from the other side. A quick examination was done on the trot. So far, so good!!

And the sweetest sound could be heard in the distance- the sound of rotors.

Within minutes the Balli was evacuated. However, the wait was to continue.

Around midday, the message came in. The Balli would live to fight another day.

War cries that would chill the enemy's spine reverberated from the defended posts.

It had taken more than 15 teams of 4 men each, over 11 hours, across treacherous mountain tracks, in pitch darkness and inclement weather, to get their man to safety.

Teamwork at its best was as infectious as it could get.

Soon, the battalion was back to work. Preparing for another busy day in the office. And it had started snowing again.

Postscript

The Major would go on leave the following year after about 13 months on the Saddle. Till then, he continued his battle.

The Balli was back in action after three months. This time everything was different. The Balli declared war on the

Pirate and the Monk and banished them from his life forever. He continued singing, but another tune and other songs. This time his favourite haunt was the religious functions on Sunday mornings. This was the least the Balli could do!

Many believed that this had to happen. It was said that on that fateful night, the Balli had met the Great Guru, the Wisest Sage of them all, who refused to take him.

Some were in awe of the Balli, for they believed that only the truly blessed could have gone into the long dark tunnel of no return and come back alive!

FAREWELL MY FRIEND

The Shadows on the Wall

Hospitals always exuded a feeling of dread and gloominess. We settled down outside the ICU for the long wait that would follow. Considering the age of the patient, hope seemed distant. It was a time to wait and watch and pray.

The shadows lengthened as darkness set in and the visitors dwindled. The long corridors looked deserted except for a few doctors and nursing staff walking around at intervals.

Finally, we were all alone in a long hall. The sick and the dying were in the adjacent rooms to give us company. Along with the spirits of the long departed, waiting in the shadows.

Then, I saw the old man huddled in one corner of the long hall, alone in the darkness. He looked familiar. I recognized him. The pilot.

The Invisible People

I used to meet the pilot on my evening walks.

Evening walks were more of a socializing trip around the colony. Saying hello to the small community of residents and tenants.

I would see the old ones sitting all alone in different corners. Sitting on cement chairs. A much-needed break for some rest before moving on. Some of them looked broken and withered. Some would be accompanied by a younger companion, probably a nurse. Some of them would wave and smile.

These men had fought battles in the air, the sea, and the land. The men and their women. A different time and place. Men and women for whom few were too many. They had lived a life far from ordinary.

They were the invisible people.

Looking for the Summer

About six decades ago, they had first met. The Academy was a cauldron of the young starry-eyed boys yet to become men. They came from different walks of life. Bonds would be made to last a lifetime.

The two cadets went on to join the Army as an Infantryman and the other as a pilot. The Infantryman was at least two years older and senior than the pilot.

As time passed, I started seeing more of these titans. The pilot was one among them. Erudite and soft-spoken, he had several stories and anecdotes.

The pilot started his commissioned life as a bomber pilot. Soon he graduated to other aircraft till he settled down to become a reconnaissance pilot. This was a time when one of the primary resources for obtaining intelligence came from air photographs. Huge and heavy cameras were strapped to slow-moving aircraft flying low over the enemy defences, making numerous turns to get the requisite pictures. The haze over the subcontinent also made reconnaissance more dangerous as flights would have to be low, well within the anti-aircraft range of the enemy. A hazardous job indeed. The information sent in by these pilots during the three wars was invaluable. So too, during peacetime along the line of control.

The Infantryman joined one of the oldest Regiments in the Indian Army and fought several battles on the Western borders. I only came to know about the Infantryman from the pilot. The strong friendship and the bonds they had built over the years.

The Curse of the Invisible People

In all your journeys, you may meet these invisible people. These are the old souls not wanted by anyone. Invisible to the young and most other people. Making a life in their deserted nests. All that remained were old friends, their coursemates. Their drink buddies.

Their children have left their homes. Finding new lives across the globe. No more having a part in the lives of the oldies. They would come to visit them occasionally.

I could see the number of young people impatiently waiting outside the ICU. Putting up expressions that they thought were sombre and showing concern about the invisible people. A quick visit and back to their routine lives.

Most of the children were rich, and they would justify their actions by claiming that the Invisibles were getting the best medical aid. Was it so?

I'll Light a Candle for You

The Infantryman was in his eighties. He had been ill for some time, yet he had plodded on. One day he collapsed and had to be evacuated to the hospital by his neighbours. Only the pilot came to meet him.

All that remained for the old Infantryman was his friend, the pilot, keeping a lone vigil throughout the night in the cold, along with the spirits of the long departed. Night after night, the pilot sat huddled in one corner of the long empty hall. Waiting for his friend to regain consciousness.

Then one night, the pilot was called by the duty doctor. His friend had regained consciousness. The Infantryman opened his eyes and looked at the pilot. He nodded in recognition. Unsaid words. Then he lapsed into a coma.

A few relatives peeped in a day later. The children were informed. It was unlikely they could visit their old man in time.

The Infantryman passed away into a great beyond two days later. Only the pilot was there.

THE VALLEY ACROSS THE RIVER

Bad Day on Saddle Hill

The sporadic enemy movement was visible on the downward reaches of the Southern slope of Saddle Hill, the Tactical Headquarters. The remnants of the battalion sat there, spread over the other two spurs of the Saddle Hill, awaiting further orders that, in all probability, would never arrive. The possibility of reinforcements coming in also seemed remote.

The enemy had crawled up over successive nights along the slopes. It was a matter of time before the enemy would close all our options.

The only access for the defenders was the narrow spur running to the Southeast. The other battalions of the Division held on in strength across the river line.

The enemy had disrupted communications at least a week before. A few stragglers coming in from the forward defences painted a grim picture. Wave after wave of enemy attacks destroyed the forward-defended posts. The defenders were either dead or taken prisoner. So too, the Brigade Headquarters. West of the Saddle Hill.

The moon was in the third quarter. The enemy was sure to attack in the night. We had to make our move before that.

Riding the Whirlwind

While the nation's attention was glued westward to its traditional foe, newfound friends became foes. The only buffer nation between the countries ceased to exist. The City of Gods was destroyed and ransacked.

Soon a series of events would catapult the young fledgling nation into a war in the Himalayas. The religious head of the buffer nation and his entourage took sanctuary with the only friend they had.

The forward policy of holding scattered posts in a terrain over 15000 feet ASL with few men on an imaginary border was to prove disastrous. Scattered posts meant poorly maintained defences. The temperatures dipped below minus for a significant part of the year.

War raged, and these forward posts ran out of ammunition quickly. Air support did not exist. So too, the reinforcements.

The battalion was enjoying the warm weather along the Ravi not too long ago. The battalion had just finished celebrating a win in the athletics competition, and the celebrations carried on into the early morning hours. That night the orders were received. Move to the Eastern Himalayas, to the land of dawn-lit mountains. The battalion moved by air with only essential equipment. Rear parties would haul the heavy luggage by land later.

No Place for An Old Man

The Old Man sat on the vantage point and tried to see and observe as much as possible. As the war progressed, the man had aged considerably. Though he was pushing forty, he looked at least ten years older. The pain in his knee had worsened. As he wobbled up to the Operations Room bunker, he had made up his mind.

The briefing was simple and straight. The remnants of the battalion were to withdraw to the river line and break out to the valley on the other side. It was a tactical withdrawal, after all. Without food, ammunition, and other essential supplies holding on to the defences made no sense. The Old Man now entrusted the entire operation to his senior-most Major, a young man yet to turn thirty.

The younger man was among the few still alive and free among the officers.

The Old Man had shed his ego. It was his sole responsibility to get his men to safety. He knew he could not do it on his own. The tasking was simple. Get them all back safely.

He would follow the leader now and not interfere with the Major's decisions. The Old Man recognized that the Major had a strong desire to survive. In any combat, the Major would give no quarter.

The Major drew up his plans. The men would move at last light. Booby-trap the equipment and supplies left behind. Mines were scattered along the enemy's path to delay progress.

The Old Man had a last look at his Operations Room. He had spent the previous few months in this room, except when he went to sleep in an adjacent bunker called the Tiger's Residence.

The Lone Rider

The young Major was lucky to be alive and had escaped becoming a prisoner twice. He reached the Tactical Headquarters with a few men and many stragglers he could rescue after a week's walk avoiding enemy patrols. Some of the men were locals, and they foraged for edible fruits and plants along the way.

Tired, the Major's party had crawled to join the Tactical Headquarters. The Old Man recognized there was no one better to take them to the river head and beyond into safety.

The Major recognized that the Old Man had made a sensible decision and respected him even more. The Old Man had briefed the Major in his bunker. The Major would take all decisions. No questions asked. The Old Man would take sole responsibility in case their plan failed.

The Major spent his time assessing his plan of action. The sick and wounded were another area of concern. The Old Man and the Doc would take responsibility for the wounded.

The only other officer in the group was a Lieutenant fresh from the Academy. The youngster would lead the battalion with a section of the fittest men. The Old Man and the sick and wounded would follow. The Major and his party would booby-trap the bunkers and bring up the rear.

The River Trail

As darkness fell, the men moved out. The men were moving light with their weapons, ammunition, and whatever was left to eat. Maintaining silence was the critical factor. It was a matter of time before the enemy would get alerted.

The river trail was about ten kilometres and followed a long, winding track that would take the men to a boat loading point.

Getting out of the enemy's automatic weapons range before midnight was also essential. By then, the men would be on the other side of the narrow ridge line. The dense foliage would give the men adequate cover from sight and movement.

The boat loading point was sure to be on the enemy's mortar targets. Getting on to boats at that point would also be risky. It was essential to have alternate plans once they reached the river line.

The entire area was sparsely populated. The few villages along the river trail were uninhabited. The locals fled once the war had commenced.

The men knew the route well. The leave parties followed the trail to the boat loading point. They would catch the ferry to cross the river. From thereon, it was approximately a three-day walk on a fair-weather track to the nearest road head. Then, another day's journey by bus to reach the rail head. The walk back was always pleasant as it meant going home for a few days of hard-earned leave. Returning from leave was never an enjoyable experience.

The battalion had reduced to one-fifth is the original size: just about a hundred and fifty fighting men and about sixty wounded. Most of the injured could hobble around except a handful that needed stretchers. That would mean tying down at least four men for each stretcher. The progress of the column would depend on the stretcher-bearing parties.

The Bend in the River

The youngster and his advance party were moving fast. They had a few tasks lined up. They were to observe and report. The presence of the enemy at the boat loading point was a distinct possibility. In such an eventuality, find an alternate boat loading point and secure it.

The advance party had taken a few detours to avoid the villages. The progress was monitored continuously by the Major. The Advance party also signposted the detours by carefully marking trees. Only a trained eye, especially someone looking for such a sign, would notice it.

The advance party reached the river head well in time. As foreseen, there were signs of enemy presence—the charred remnants of boats scattered on the banks of the river.

The youngster decided to move upstream. Logic dictated that the river would be shallower upstream. The depth of the water meant that crossing would be more accessible, and rafts would be required only for the wounded.

For the next 48 hours, the weather would hold. So far, so good. Flash floods could change the course of action and make crossing precarious.

They found a suitable place further above the bend in the river—approximately a couple of kilometres from the initially planned crossing point, it was defiladed from the tracks. The advance party took up defences and waited for the remainder column.

Blood on the Moon

The enemy attacked around midnight. The Major's party had a clear two-hour advantage. They had reached the top of the adjoining spur line when they saw the explosions on Saddle Hill. Not waiting to find out, they raced to join the Old Man's group.

The reserve echelons of the enemy moved in hot pursuit. Enemy mortars started firing at all their previously registered targets. Most of these targets were the crossings close to the deserted villages.

The progress of the column slowed down and almost came to a standstill. The wounded and the stretcher borne were the worst affected. By then, the Major's party had caught up with them.

It was here the detours helped the column. Taking a break was out of the question. The first light was a few hours away. Stopping now would mean disaster.

Slowly the column reached the new rendezvous. The Advance party had managed to rig up a raft for the stretchers. Each trip could take two or three stretchers at the most—at least three to four visits by ferry.

Within half an hour, most of the column had waded across. The Major and his group had taken up defences around the crossing point.

The enemy announced their arrival with accurate small-arms fire. Mortars pounded the banks of the river.

The Divisional Headquarters had received information about the battalion. All hell broke loose as the defences across the river opened up. The heavy artillery, mortars and heavy machine guns were firing in tandem. As they made merry, the enemy beat a retreat.

The major and his men picked up the wounded and quickly waded across the river.

The Men and the Mission

Leaders need to display confidence in themselves and the men they lead. At times leaders must accept that they may not be the best suited for a particular job. It takes guts to take decisions to get the job done.

Leadership is getting the best out of the men, never forgetting the overall mission.

THE GODS SMILED

Time to Begin

I peddled away furiously on my buddy's bicycle in the darkness. The black tarmac was visible just a few feet ahead of me. Dawn seemed so far away. The Company jeep that was supposed to pick me up had developed a mechanical fault and left me stranded.

Close to the start point, I could see a few hurricane lanterns lit up to illuminate the start point. I could also see the outline of a couple of 180-pounder tents on one side of the road. There were just a handful of officials. On the other side of the road were a few members of various teams. The race had just commenced a few minutes before. I decided to wait and watch the proceedings.

The Preparations

The days of routine peacetime activity. It was two years since the Battalion had moved into this sleepy town bordering the Thar. Later that year, we were to move to a new location along the Kalidhar for another tour of active duty.

Summers were blisteringly hot, and winters chillingly cold. In severe winters, the water left out in buckets would form a thin ice crust. Otherwise, the weather was dry throughout the year. If ever it rained, it would get unusually humid.

In such times, life's monotony was best broken by competition. Competitions are good and can bring out the best of us. It also allowed the Commanding Officers to prove their mettle.

It was almost the end of February. Not too cold or warm. The time before the onset of summer. Time for the first competition of the season.

The preparations had begun in earnest. Teams from various battalions were training hard. Some were new, having moved into the cantonment that year. A few were on their way out, coming to the end of their three-year peacetime stay. Each one was hoping to make a mark and prove themselves. We were part of the latter group, wanting to sign off in style.

The Competition

Ever since the time of Pheidippides, the marathon has been a race that holds us in awe. The modern-day standard corporate events classify all runs above a kilometre as a half marathon, 5 km marathon and whatnot.

The marathon runs over 42 kilometres or 26 miles is a severe test of human endurance. It takes a heavy toll on the runner mentally and physically.

The national record had been set by the Army man from Bihar a couple of years before this story happened. Even today, as I narrate this story, the same record stands at 2 hours and 12 minutes.

We were the reigning Champs. The Battalion had the Champ. Malkiat Singh, a naturally gifted runner, had previously participated in the National level Championships and finished in the top twenty. The man to beat.

The other battalions had some good runners. The nearest rivals were the two runners from Rajasthan and Bihar. Younger and with the sole mission of beating the Champ.

The teams were all fielding more than two or three runners. The Battalion did not have any reserves. There was one long-distance runner who had never been tried out.

Chamkaur Singh the reserve - Silent, unseen, and unheard. He was from the Champ's neighbouring district. The man was of medium height and always appeared gloomy. I got to know the reasons later.

For this narrative, I shall refer to Malkiat Singh as the Champ and Chamkaur Singh as the Challenger.

The Best Laid Plans

I was part of the sports team with no defined responsibilities. I was asked to motivate and mentally tune the runners. I decided to observe the runners before deciding on a course of action.

I spoke to the team captain, my senior subaltern, and the team trainer. They did not seem to be happy to talk of the Challenger. He was the "pretender' to the title. Each team needed to field a minimum of two runners. There was only one option to include the reserve.

The team strategy was simple. The Champ would play second fiddle till halftime as the Challenger was to set the pace. After crossing the halfway point, the Champ would take over. He had the experience and the capability to run such a tactical race. It was only logical that the team was banking on their trump card. Sacrificing a pawn to achieve the overall objective was justified.

The competition was a few days away, so it was time to talk to both. I could see the disdain in the Champ's eyes for the Challenger. I had to meet up with each one separately.

The Champ was in sync with the team plan. He was the Champ and the Ace in the pack. He knew what had to be done and exuded confidence.

The Challenger also seemed upbeat. He told me that he had never had a chance over the years, and this was his first and probably his last competitive race. The Battalion was to move out that year, and the tour of active duty meant an end to these peacetime competitions. The Challenger had already crossed his thirtieth year and did not foresee himself running any more marathons.

He was aware of the team's strategy. He kept the same demeanour, yet his eyes seemed to be smiling.

So far, the overall strategy has looked good. What could go wrong?

It Never Rains Here

It was still dark when the race got off. The skies were heavily overcast. It had become unusually humid too.

For what seemed an eternity, there was no news about the runners. The sun had risen, and it was broad daylight. Just near the halfway mark, tragedy struck.

The PRC radio set with the medical backup team trailing the runners in an ambulance was the only means of communication about the progress of the run. Suddenly, the radio set crackled. A message came in that a few of the runners had become casualties. The casualties needed to be evacuated immediately to the Military hospital.

About twenty minutes later, the ambulance sped across the start point without stopping. There were no updates, no news about what had happened.

It was now more than two hours since the race had started. The first runner appeared across the wide bend in the road. He was now sprinting the last kilometre or so to the finish point. There was no one close to him. The other runners still needed to catch up.

The runners came closer, and I was dumbstruck by what I saw. It was the Challenger, the man whom no one had ever given a chance to finish in the top ten. Chamkaur Singh had a sizeable lead over the rest. He had also set a record for the division.

What had happened that day? Slowly things started falling into place. I spoke to Chamkaur Singh to get the complete story.

The Fall Guy

The man was the Champ now. Yet he had a troubled past and his share of suffering.

Ridiculed for his humble origins and ostracized in his village, he sought a way out. He assumed that life in the Battalion would be different. Life in the Battalion was better as he got enough to eat, a decent salary and a feeling of belonging.

Yet life was no different for him here from his village. The discrimination followed in various forms. Sometimes village rivalries, jealousies, and biases spill onto daily life. Though Malkiat Singh had enrolled much after Chamkaur Singh, he had got promoted earlier and had become senior to the latter. It also did not help that Chamkaur Singh was also a long-distance runner.

The team strategy made Chamkaur Singh the fall guy. It gave Malkiat Singh a chance to win. Chamkaur Singh had started the race with the team strategy in mind. This was his last race, and he wanted to finish in glory.

After about three miles of tarred road, the route shifted to a desert track. The desert track was well defined by the regular traffic of camel carts and occasional four-wheelers. The trail wound its way across dunes, skirted around the largest dune in that area, and then went back to join the tarred road.

Once the race progressed, Chamkaur Singh set a blistering pace. He was accustomed to such conditions. He had been running on sand and muddy tracks back home near the Ravi. As he pounded the desert track, the years of humiliation and anger felt like it was flowing out. He thought he was riding the wind. The Champ and the others tried their best to keep up. It was getting difficult every minute as the lead kept increasing.

On the home stretch, he saw some of his company mates cheering. Egged on, he moved faster.

Sometimes one needs to factor in the weather conditions. It is strange that when luck turns your way, even nature stops to help you.

What happened next is conjecture. Was Malkiat Singh overconfident? Or did he have a late night? Or was it that the Champ was about to lose to the man he had held in contempt for a long time? Or was the excess humidity that got to him, and he collapsed?

Three more of the leading pack also collapsed, done in by dehydration.

With no worthwhile opposition left, the fall guy was now the undisputed leader of the pack.

Ode to the New Champ

The Battalion had achieved its aim. We would sign off in style. Unbeaten in the marathon event during our three-year stay in this sleepy old town bordering the Thar.

Malkiat Singh was humbled. Badly shaken, he was quick to get back on track. Gone were the swag and the loud banter. He was chosen to lead the divisional team for the marathon. The team management felt this was a one-off failure for him; Chamkaur Singh was seen as a flash in the pan and not considered for the team. Strange, indeed, are the ways humans think and draw judgements. Some never get due credit for their efforts and are consigned to remain in darkness.

For Chamkaur Singh, it was the last race he ever ran. He went off with the advance party in early autumn to the new location in the mountains to the North.

He was back to his quiet self, yet his eyes had a strange lustre.

I never met him again as I was commanding another company. I came to know, much later, that he had taken early retirement and returned to his village. He later enrolled in the State police.

Chamkaur Singh owned the world on that eventful day, having defeated his nemesis.

For some, an opportunity comes once in a Lifetime. How we grasp these fleeting moments depends entirely on us.

DELIVERANCE

The Watcher

It was a cold December evening. The shadows had started lengthening. I again noticed the tall man standing across the street. He just kept watching the soldiers inside the makeshift Army camp.

He was dressed the same way I had seen him the previous week. His turban was perfect, and his flowing white beard was left unkempt. His jacket was old yet good enough to protect him from the cold. He would come around late afternoon and always stand at the same place and look at the soldiers and the civilian visitors standing in a line wanting to speak to me. He would leave a few hours later.

I decided it was time to make my move. I crossed the gate and went to meet the watcher. He looked at me, nodded his head and walked away.

The Camp

The last decade of the previous century saw the State limping back to peace after a few years of turmoil and unrest. A new future beckoned with elections scheduled for the coming summer. The battalion headquarters with the company I was commanding had moved into a small town in the East of Punjab that year. It was about a fortnight since we had set our base in one of the marketplaces commonly found. The campsite was a series of tents with a barbed-wire fence to demarcate a boundary.

The troops did not seem happy being in their home state. It was not the best time to be involved in "aid to civil authorities". The State was in transition. The wounds had not healed yet. Far too many things had happened in recent memory. Yet being good soldiers, we had to focus on the tasks.

The weather was also changing fast. Frost and fog, and intermittent rains added to our woes. Apart from regular soldiering, the fraternization program kept me busy. I was meeting various civilians wanting a speedy resolution to their problems. After the initial rush, the number of visitors became a trickle, except those still searching for their loved ones- the ones gone missing.

The next day, the sentry at the main gate informed me that a senior veteran wanted to meet me. It was the watcher. He wished to talk to me.

After a formal introduction, we started talking. The veteran spoke. I kept listening.

The Veteran

He was an infantryman in his late 70s. He had been part of the operations in Burma, wounded and decorated for gallantry. Pegu, Sittang and Irrawaddy. He had seen it all. Post-independence, he fought in the '47 and '62 operations. In 1963, he decided he had had enough of battle and retired to look after the farm and family. He earned an honorary commission just before he retired.

He was able to educate his children well. The eldest daughter and son had migrated to Canada a decade ago. His story was about the other two sons, especially the youngest one -the son born to the veteran in the autumn of his life.

The late 70s and early 80s saw a period of intense turbulence in the State. The siege of the Temple devastated the community. The veteran said that there was a call for arms. He had to choose between Country and Community.

What a predicament to be in! To choose sides or to walk the tightrope? Whatever his choice, it would condemn him and continue haunting him until he lived. Past sacrifices were of no significance now.

The veteran said, "I was speechless when the elder one decided to pitch his lot with the religious movement. I could see that the only ending would be violent and sorrowful. The moment I knew that I had lost him forever. "

Time passed. The veteran went back to farming. The youngest son got his call letter to join his father's regiment. He left home, promising his mother that he would get his elder brother to return home. That was the last they saw of him. Eight years had passed since that day.

The veteran wanted me to find his younger son. My heart went out to this wizened soldier. I said that I would try to find his son.

The Bond

Over the next few months, the veteran became a regular visitor to the campsite. Though separated by more than a generation, we bonded well. Soldiers share a bond wherever they are. After all, he had spent a lifetime fighting for our country, narrowly escaping death repeatedly. We also prayed to the same God.

As the days went by, I listened to his stories and experiences. I gained a lot by listening to him and drawing my lessons. He gave me tips on company administration.

He told me about his young Company Commander and the battle where the officer had died saving a young soldier. How he and his platoon carried out the last rites and buried him in a grave in Burma.

His stories told me about the importance of building relationships. I learnt that those transactional relations are transitory– and the need to go that extra bit.

Meanwhile, I received my posting orders. I had to leave within a week. Events started moving fast. The superintendent of police had become a good friend by then and told me that he had gotten some leads on this case.

I decided to visit the veteran before I moved out of the station.

The Old Woman

The veteran had a sprawling house amid the fields in a nearby village. Coming from a traditional land-owning family, he was affluent. He seemed happy to meet me. He told me he had learned I would be leaving the place soon. The soldiers in the campsite had told him.

There, I met his wife. She sat motionless on a chair facing the window in her room with no expression. She seemed to be watching the track leading to her house.

She had been like that for a long time now. She was in a world of her own.

The woman had sorrow writ on her face. She did not utter a word. I learned that she had not spoken a word since that inauspicious day.

I tried speaking to her. I was curious to know if she heard or understood anything I said. Ultimately, I told her I would find out about her son before I left the campsite. I would certainly meet her again with some news.

As I was leaving, I thought I saw a glimpse of a smile across her face. Or was it my imagination- I was not sure?

Tell Me There's a Heaven

Early the following day, I left for the capital, a few hours away. A representative of the superintendent accompanied me. The fog made movement slow and hazardous. I reached the Headquarters around 930am. The contact in the Headquarters was already waiting for me. She had got a few relevant files from that period ready. I had time till 10 am to get the information I wanted. After that, the offices would start filling in.

Amidst one of the voluminous files, I got the story of the elder son. I glanced through the file and got to the last page. There was also a footnote about an identified youth. As I closed the file, the wall clock chimed 10 am. I slowly got up and left. I was devastated by what I had discovered. Sad and heavy-hearted, I reached the camp late in the afternoon.

I kept thinking about it. I could not make any sense of this case. Why did the veteran not tell me everything?

The next day I decided to meet the veteran and his wife and speak to them.

The house seemed deserted. The veteran was waiting for me. Before I could say anything, he broke down and wept like a child. After some time, which seemed like an eternity, he said, "She passed away yesterday at about 10 am. We cremated her yesterday only.

"Before you say anything, let me fill you with the details. I came to your camp with a lot of anger and bitterness. When I saw you doing your work, I decided to meet you.

"I got a reception I never expected. As I kept talking to you, the anger in me started melting. I told you a part of the story to gain your attention. I never reminded you about it again. I started feeling at ease after a long time. I knew I had to keep coming to find some inner peace. I thought that I was back in a place that seemed like home.

"Yet, I failed to realize that I had underestimated you. I did not expect you to go after the truth.

"The day after my younger son left the house, I got the message that my elder son died in an encounter. My wife was inconsolable. She went into a depression that very moment. She stopped speaking and went into a shell.

"I left home to the spot and received the body of my elder son. I also learnt that an unidentified youth had died in the crossfire. There were no records or identification whatsoever on the young man.

"It was by chance that the belongings of that unidentified youth caught my attention. That day I received two bodies- of both my sons. I still do not know what happened that day. I never told anyone about my younger son, not even my wife. Please do not ask me anything anymore.

"After you left my house, my wife seemed cheerful. It was after such a long time. She spoke to me late into the night of times gone by and our children. She looked forward to meeting her son. Yesterday, she woke up early and made breakfast. We ate together. She sat on her chair. And then suddenly she passed away."

How could a man endure so much suffering? How did he carry this burden for such a long time? I sat there for some more time silently. As the sun set, I dragged myself away, leaving the veteran.

He said, "I do not know if I will meet you again. Thank you for everything. I am happy that my wife died peacefully!"

Deliverance

The truth may not necessarily bring you peace of mind, nor may it set you free. It can catch you by the throat or confine you into a prison of your making.

For the old woman, it was deliverance. She had finally found eternal peace and united with her sons.

For the veteran, it was a fate I would not choose for anyone. The proud soldier was making his last stand as he had now broken out of prison. He would go to his grave with all his secrets, carrying a burden he could not share with anyone.

Would I be ever free, for I had lost a friend? Sometimes I see my friend appearing through the fog, standing across the street, and watching me. I know he wants to talk to me.

I get up to go across and welcome him.

And, like the first time, he would nod at me and disappear into the fog.

9 789357 415774